CW00545644

CANTERBURY
THEN & NOW

IN COLOUR

PAUL CRAMPTON

The
History
Press

First published in 2011

The History Press
The Mill, Brimscombe Port
Stroud, Gloucestershire, GL5 2QG
www.thehistorypress.co.uk

ISBN 978 0 7524 6296 7

Typesetting and origination by The History Press
Printed in India
Manufacturing managed by Jellyfish Print Solutions Ltd

CONTENTS

ACKNOWLEDGEMENTS

I would like to thank Derek Butler, John Clark, Gerry Whittaker and Ted Yeoman for supplying photographic material. A special vote of thanks must also go to the photographers whose work appears herein. They are: Patrick Brown, David Cousins, Mr R.E. Cranfield, Bill Entwhistle, Kenneth Gravett, Mr A. Moody, Barrie Stretch, Dr William Urry, Rob Williams and Edward Wilmot.

My final word of appreciation goes to those who allowed me to use material from their archives: Barrett's of Canterbury, Canterbury Archaeological Trust, Canterbury Local Study Collection, Canterbury Museums, English Heritage and the *Kentish Gazette*.

ABOUT THE AUTHOR

After twenty-eight years in a salaried job for BT, Paul Crampton took early retirement in order to pursue his passion to write fiction and non-fiction books, as well as setting up his own online second-hand book-selling business. He owns a large archive of Canterbury photographs, many of which have never been published before.

INTRODUCTION

Some thirteen years have now passed since the first edition of *Canterbury Then & Now* was published. In that time, further changes have occurred in our city, rendering the previous 'now' photographs a little out of date. Therefore, when the opportunity to do an updated, colour version of the book, with the best forty-five 'then' and 'now' pairings, presented itself, I relished the chance to bring it into the twenty-first century.

For those of you who didn't have the first edition, this book will prove to be a dramatic record of the changes that Canterbury has seen over the last 100 years or so. However, the value of 'then' and 'now' pictures is not in the amount of time that separates them, but in the changes that are represented.

Most of our towns and cities changed more in the 1950s and 1960s than at any other time, including the Blitz. Slum clearance, road widening and the shift from public to private transport have all left their mark. Indeed, Canterbury has seen more than its fair share of changes over the years.

The bombing of 1940–42 obviously caused many unwelcome alterations to countless Canterbury streets. More importantly, though, the Blitz proved to be a catalyst for a comprehensive modernisation plan that would have changed the entire city. As it happened, two significant factors slowed the desire for such all-encompassing changes. These were a well-orchestrated local protest, fought in the 1945 elections against the City Council's plans for wide-sweeping compulsory purchase, and then the drying up of government funds in the mid 1950s. Interestingly, conservation and the desire to retain old historic buildings didn't really become a significant lobbying factor until the early 1970s, by which time the all-powerful Canterbury City Council, with its autonomous county borough status, had been consigned to history.

The needs of the ever-increasing number of motorcars became even more demanding in the 1960s. New garages and filling stations appeared and existing facilities were greatly expanded. Steam also disappeared from our railways and most goods sidings were ripped up as freight transport transferred to the roads. From the early 1970s onwards, Canterbury's main street was progressively pedestrianised, as direct private transport access to the city centre became far less of a priority. Sadly though, at the same time, many of the more useful shops – often family-run and adequately providing for our daily needs – were closed for good. Ultimately, they would be replaced by large supermarkets on the city's outskirts.

I have been passionately involved with *Canterbury Then & Now*-style projects for nearly twenty-five years, and I am happy to include this revised and updated book as among my proudest achievements.

CASTLE STREET

CASTLE STREET, PART of the main north-south route through the city, in the early 1930s. There have been a few changes in the intervening years. The eighteenth-century shop, furthest right, was a victim of the Blitz. Other buildings have since changed use, notably the pair of early nineteenth-century houses beyond the St John's Lane junction (on the right), which have since

been converted into a café and a guest house.
Further down on the left, the former Globe Public
House and Cakebread Robey premises were
demolished in the 1950s and 1970s respectively.
(Reproduced with kind permission of Ted Yeoman)

THE OPENING OF the second stage of the
city ring road in 1969 took most of the A28
through-traffic away from Castle Street. In more
recent years, it has ceased to be a thoroughfare
altogether, and is now blocked off at the bottom
end to prevent 'rat-running' to the city centre.
Despite this, many tourist coaches ignore the
'no through road' signs, and cause chaos as they
come to grief at the bollards.

ST GEORGE'S STREET

ST GEORGE'S STREET, the most prestigious section of Canterbury's main street (and part of the A2) decorated for 'Cricket Week' in the early years of last century. This scene changed almost completely following the Baedeker Raid of 1 June 1942. As a result, only the gutted shell of

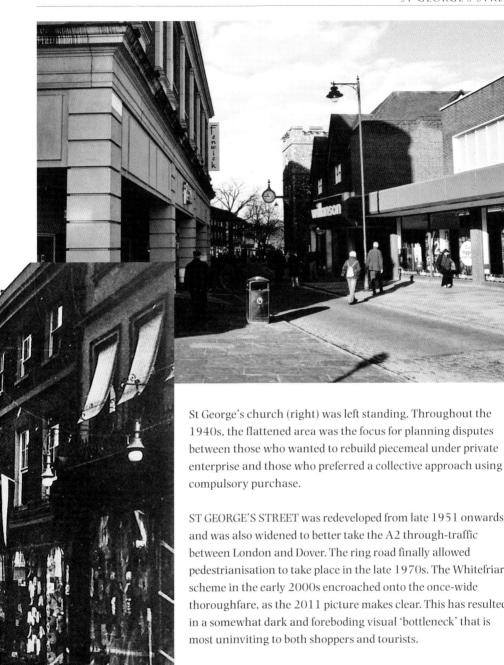

St George's church (right) was left standing. Throughout the
1940s, the flattened area was the focus for planning disputes
between those who wanted to rebuild piecemeal under private
enterprise and those who preferred a collective approach using
compulsory purchase.

ST GEORGE'S STREET was redeveloped from late 1951 onwards,
and was also widened to better take the A2 through-traffic
between London and Dover. The ring road finally allowed
pedestrianisation to take place in the late 1970s. The Whitefriars
scheme in the early 2000s encroached onto the once-wide
thoroughfare, as the 2011 picture makes clear. This has resulted
in a somewhat dark and foreboding visual 'bottleneck' that is
most uninviting to both shoppers and tourists.

ST GEORGE'S PLACE

ST GEORGE'S PLACE at dawn on 1 June 1942. A once impressive row of late Georgian buildings has been reduced to gutted shells and smouldering rubble. Here, the incendiary fires burnt almost unchecked, the National Fire Service being too busy elsewhere. In the centre of

the picture a fragmented shell is all that is left of Dr Wacher's house, one of the few properties that was still a private residence rather than having been converted into offices.
(Reproduced with kind permission of The Fisk Moore Collection)

IN THE POST-WAR development plan, St George's Place was part of an area designated for commercial use. Consequently, new buildings such as the *Kentish Gazette* premises appeared here in the 1950s. These were set back from the then existing street line to allow for later widening to a dual carriageway. This finally occurred in 1969. Today, the road is as busy as it ever was, feeding incoming traffic into Canterbury and on to the clogged city ring road.

HIGH STREET

THE CHOKED HIGH Street from the Guildhall Street junction in 1956. Bicycles, vans, a bus and a motorbike and side car are held up by parked delivery vans on both sides of the street. Later the same year, the relocation of the bus station from St Peter's Place to St George's Lane would reduce the number of buses in the main street. Then, in the 1960s, the construction of the ring road would further ease the situation, albeit temporarily.
(Reproduced with kind permission of The Fisk Moore Collection)

PEDESTRIANISATION OF THE High Street, together with The Parade and St Peter's Street, finally came in the 1980s, to coincide

with the opening of the Canterbury bypass. Vehicular access is now only given to delivery vehicles before 10.30 am and after 4.00 pm. Overall, as far as the buildings are concerned, this section of the High Street is largely as it was in the mid 1950s, although many of the actual shops now have at least one eye on the tourist industry.

UNION STREET

UNION STREET WAS one of the roads laid out in the early nineteenth century to provide housing for the families of soldiers stationed at the nearby barracks. From 1959 onwards,

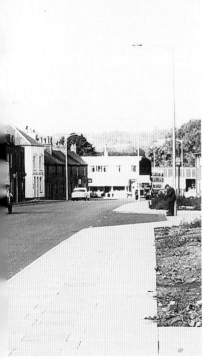

the area was subject to slum clearance. By October 1961, Union Street was in a transitional state, as pictured here. Houses on the north (right) side had been demolished and new council accommodation built. Moreover, the street itself had been considerably widened and become part of the A28 route to Thanet.
(Reproduced with kind permission of the Kentish Gazette*)*

THE OLD HOUSES on the south (left) side of the street were pulled down in 1962 and replaced by low-rise blocks of flats. Only the William IV public house survived. Union Street remained part of the national trunk road network until the 1980s, when the construction of Tourtel Road finally allowed the street to be restricted to access only. Today, the planting has matured and parking for local people is plentiful, resulting in a much-improved living environment.

WINCHEAP GREEN

THE WINCHEAP GREEN area seen from Station Road East in January 1963. Here Station Road meets Wincheap Street (left), Castle Street (centre right) and Wincheap Green itself (right), as well as the station approach road. Within months, the area would be totally transformed by the construction of Wincheap roundabout, part of the first stage of the ring road, which was opened in June 1963. All properties in the old picture were demolished. *(Reproduced with kind permission of Canterbury Museums)*

WINCHEAP ROUNDABOUT FORMED the limit of the city ring road until 1969, when the second stage was extended through to

Broad Street. Since then, the roundabout itself has been altered many times in attempts to improve the traffic flow. Unfortunately, given the present bottleneck of Wincheap itself (left of the photograph), this is unlikely to ever improve, and will remain a headache for anyone trying to get to and from work or school.

UPPER BRIDGE STREET

THIS 'THEN' PICTURE was taken to record a fire in the roof of the empty and derelict property at No. 2 Upper Bridge Street in March 1966. Beyond the fire engine is the St George's crossroads. By this time, details of the second stage of the ring road had been announced and all of these old properties were destined for demolition to make way for St George's roundabout.
(Reproduced with kind permission of the Kentish Gazette*)*

AFTER ALL THE old buildings had been swept away, the second stage of Canterbury's ring road was opened in late 1969. However, the modern 1950s buildings, seen to the far right of both photographs, had been built on an alignment that anticipated the later street improvements, so have survived to this day. St George's roundabout (to the left of the photograph above) is pictured on a quiet Sunday morning, as at any other time the photograph, taken from the central reservation, would not have been possible.

DANE JOHN MOAT

A LONE FIGURE negotiates the winding footpath along the Dane John Moat in May 1968, probably a route she has taken on countless shopping trips to the city centre. At this location, she passes an old ship's capstan and the weed-covered plinth upon which once stood a First World War tank before it was broken up for salvage in the last war. Only eighteen months later, this idyllic scene was destroyed forever. The trees were felled and the ground levelled prior to the construction of the second stage of the ring road from Wincheap Green to Broad Street.
(Reproduced with kind permission of the Kentish Gazette*)*

TODAY, A PLEASANT, almost rural walk along the alignment of the old city moat is sadly a thing of the past. Access is still possible but not encouraged. As it is, this much narrower, neatly grassed area is only brightened by the occasional tree and the all-too-brief display of daffodils in the springtime. The old ship's capstan, once thought lost, is now believed to be in a garden somewhere in the Whitstable area.

DUKES MEADOW, HARBLEDOWN

THE OLD A2 road from London passed through the ancient village of Harbledown on the last leg of its route to Canterbury. The road was narrow, hilly and winding. By the 1960s, with vehicles, especially lorries, increasing in size, weight and quantity, the traffic situation became very difficult. Delays were common, accidents frequent and damage by vehicles to property was a regular occurrence. Relief finally came in the early 1970s with the building of Harbledown bypass. The old picture (right) from May 1973 shows Dukes Meadow with surveyors' poles already in place.
(*Reproduced with kind permission of the* Kentish Gazette)

SHORTLY AFTER THE group of councillors and road contract officials had walked the proposed route of the bypass, construction work began in earnest. Given the sloping nature of the land – a favourite sledging location for generations of local children – a cutting had to be made at this location, and then a shallow embankment further down the route. With these problems, it was only possible to construct a single-carriageway road. The current picture was taken from a pedestrian overbridge.

THE REGAL CINEMA

AN ILLUSTRATION OF the impressive symmetrical façade of the new Regal Cinema in subdued art deco style. It was taken from a souvenir booklet published to commemorate

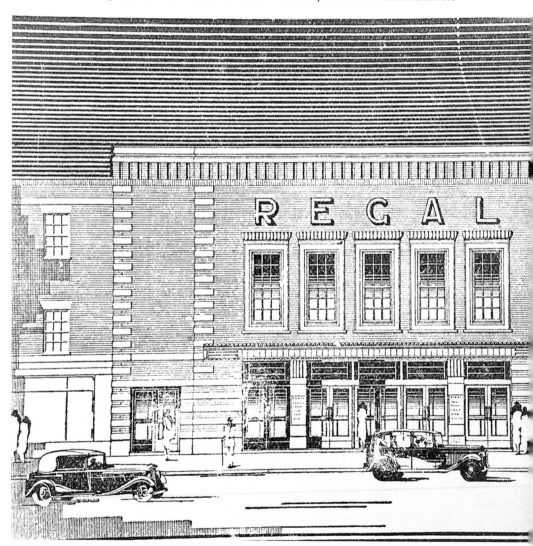

the Silver Jubilee of King George V in 1935. The well-balanced proportions of the cinema frontage lasted only until October 1942, when a bomb destroyed the Regal ballroom to the right and part of the main cinema façade. Those in the long queue waiting to see *Gone With the Wind* had a lucky escape.

THE SURVIVING TWO-THIRDS of the Regal were repaired at the end of the 1940s and the void to the right of the building was bricked off. The result was a somewhat lop-sided frontage, which can clearly be seen in the picture above. A plan to rebuild the ballroom in the early 1960s came to nothing because the land needed (right) had been earmarked for the ring road. Recent plans have identified the area for comprehensive redevelopment, so the truncated cinema may soon see its doors closed for good.

THE OLD MARLOWE THEATRE

THE SAD SIGHT of the original Marlowe Theatre in St Margaret's Street being demolished in June 1982 (right) to make way for a shopping development. The theatre had been converted from an old cinema and opened in 1951. Many famous personalities and bands have appeared here over the years, notably Pink Floyd in March 1969. The new Marlowe Theatre found a home in another redundant cinema, the Odeon in The Friars, which was extensively altered for the purpose.

(Reproduced with kind permission of the Kentish Gazette)

THE SECOND MARLOWE Theatre, adapted from the former Odeon cinema in The Friars, has itself since been demolished in order to give way to the larger Marlowe mark three, on the same site. Meanwhile, back on the Rose Lane, St Margaret's Street site, the early 1980s Marlowe Shopping Arcade has recently undergone extensive refurbishment, particularly to the Rose Lane frontage, as can be seen in the photograph above.

BURGATE STREET

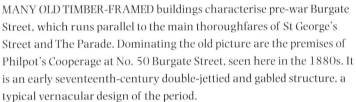

MANY OLD TIMBER-FRAMED buildings characterise pre-war Burgate Street, which runs parallel to the main thoroughfares of St George's Street and The Parade. Dominating the old picture are the premises of Philpot's Cooperage at No. 50 Burgate Street, seen here in the 1880s. It is an early seventeenth-century double-jettied and gabled structure, a typical vernacular design of the period.

THE JUNE 1942 Blitz comprehensively swept away all the old buildings along this stretch of Burgate. Redevelopment, in the flat-roofed modernist style, finally came to the site in the late 1950s. These somewhat rudimentary shops were themselves demolished in the early 2000s, and replaced by a much larger-scale development, which superficially draws its inspiration from the buildings lost to the Luftwaffe's bombs so long ago.

THE BUTTER MARKET AND CHRIST CHURCH GATE

THE WELL-KNOWN Buttermarket at the end of the last century (opposite). Three of Canterbury's secondary streets converge here, namely Burgate Street, Mercery Lane and Sun Street. The famous Marlowe Memorial, erected here in 1891, dominates the scene. Soaring up behind is the battered and weathered Christ Church Gate, the main entrance to Canterbury Cathedral. In 1921, the Marlowe Memorial was moved to Dane John, to make way for the city's First World War memorial. This can be seen in the current view, below. The gateway was restored in stages during the 1930s.

THE TURRETS OF Christ Church Gate were the last element of the restoration plan to be completed. Then, in the 1980s, a figure of Christ was installed above the main entrance, in a niche that had remained vacant since the Reformation. The Buttermarket itself has also seen many changes over the years, briefly becoming a car park in the 1950s. These days, the tables of the Olive Branch pub often occupy the space, although at the time of writing, roadworks are preventing this.

LADY WOOTTON'S GREEN
AND BROAD STREET

LADY WOOTTON'S GREEN in the 1890s (opposite), looking towards the city wall and cathedral beyond. Originally, the lane led directly to Findon Gate and St Augustine's Abbey, behind the camera. To the left is a delightful pair of seventeenth-century cottages, outside which an elderly woman is clearing the footpath. Further down is a short terrace of eighteenth-century houses fronting Broad Street and standing between the two branches of Lady Wootton's Green.

IN THE 1920s, the cottages fronting Broad Street were demolished and a small formal garden was laid out between the two branches of Lady Wootton's Green. Later, in 1942, the seventeenth-century houses (left of the old view) were cleared away following extensive Blitz damage. After a lengthy period as a muddy car park, the blitzed site immediately adjoining Lady Wootton's Green was redeveloped with a row of neo-Georgian terraced houses in the mid to late 1950s.

KING STREET

KING STREET RUNS in a north to south direction parallel to the main shopping thoroughfare of Palace Street for much of its length. Unlike its grander neighbour, it has always been mostly residential and used by traffic gaining access to the adjacent lanes. The old picture from 1938 shows Nos 24–27 intact and the remains of No. 23, following the clearance of much of Knotts Lane to the left. These King Street properties were empty by 1940 and demolished in 1946. *(Reproduced with kind permission of Dr William Urry)*

MUCH OF THE King Street-Knotts Lane slum clearance area was not redeveloped in the early post-war years, as the land was earmarked for the north to south cross-city relief road. In any event, public conveniences were built on this corner site in the mid 1950s. At the time of writing, they have been closed for some time, and demolition to make way for housing is once more in the offing.

THE FINDON GATE

THE FINDON GATE in Monastery Street, seen from Lady Wootton's Green a few days after the main air raid of 1 June 1942 (left). Although not actually hit, the old gateway, once the main access to St Augustine's Abbey, was badly damaged by the blast. There was so much damage to the stone facing of its northern (left) tower that the structure had to be shored up until after the war. *(Reproduced with kind permission of The Fisk Moore Collection)*

RESTORATION AND REPAIR of Findon Gate was completed in 1947, although the stone used in this process has not weathered-in well, and still stands out somewhat starkly. In recent years, the Lady Wootton's Green garden area, seen in the foreground, has been graced by the additional of large statues depicting King Ethelbert and Queen Bertha, the latter of which can be seen in the above view.

IRON BAR LANE

ARCHAEOLOGIST MR SHEPPARD FRERE (left) oversees the mechanical clearance of a large bomb site, between Iron Bar Lane and Canterbury Lane, in the summer of 1949. Designated

'Area R', the site subsequently yielded a small sixteenth-century cellar and the junction of two Roman city roads. Parked cars and a blitzed garage in the narrow Iron Bar Lane can be seen beyond the tree saplings and buddleia. Post-war redevelopment of the area began in 1952.

THE EARLY 1950S redevelopment process saw Iron Bar Lane considerably widened, and a new lane, appropriately named Link Lane, laid out between it and the parallel Canterbury Lane. The immediate locale then became an unloading area for all the new shops in the vicinity. Plain flat-roofed shops finally lined Iron Bar Lane in the late 1950s. Those on the lane's west side gave way to a larger development in the early 2000s, while those on the east side, nearest the camera in the above view, are still hanging on.

ST RADIGUND'S STREET

ST RADIGUND'S STREET in 1957, a quiet residential road in the north of the city. In medieval times it ran along the inside of the city wall. Many of its houses and buildings were constructed following the demolition of the wall here in the late eighteenth and early nineteenth centuries. Post-war plans for Canterbury were destined to change St Radigund's Street greatly. It was to become a dual carriageway and part of the city's ring road.

HAVING BEEN BLIGHTED by the ring road (stage three), much advance demolition occurred on both sides of St Radigund's Street. Temporary

car parks were set up in the gaps between the surviving houses. A multi-storey car park for this immediate area was also added to the city development plans in the 1960s. In the event, both ring road and multi-storey plans had been dropped by the end of 1975. Subsequent residential redevelopment has returned the street to something like its 1950s appearance.

STOUR STREET

THE OLD VIEW, from September 1960, was taken at the top end of Stour Street, opposite the tannery. It shows two old buildings soon to be pulled down. The seventeenth-century jettied house was replaced by the Rosemary Lane car park and the early nineteenth-century brick house made way for an extension to the gardens of the nearby almshouse. Early 1970s plans to turn

Stour Street into a wide access road to a proposed lorry unloading
area were thankfully dropped.
(Reproduced with kind permission of Kenneth Gravett)

BY THE MID 2000s, Stour Street began to see another round of
changes. A new residential development finally appeared on the site
of the lost seventeenth- and nineteenth-century houses, as can be
seen in the current picture. Meanwhile, opposite these, the former
tannery site was gradually transformed into a massive housing
complex, re-employing some of the old buildings. At the time of
writing, those fronting Stour Street had yet to be converted.

ROSE LANE

THE 'RED DEAN' of Canterbury Cathedral, Hewlett Johnson, holds a
C.N.D. banner as he leads a good-natured protest march out of Rose
Lane, across Watling Street and on to the City Council offices at the Dane
John in February 1960. While the marchers are the photographer's
intended subject, the buildings on either side of the narrow Rose
Lane junction are of equal interest. The typewriter shop (right) was
demolished in 1961 and the grocer's shop (left) in 1962.
(*Reproduced with kind permission of the* Kentish Gazette)

FOLLOWING THE AFOREMENTIONED demolition in the early 1960s,
Rose Lane was widened to become a processional way linking the

cathedral with a proposed Civic Centre development on the Dane John. This plan was dropped in 1968, although Rose Lane remained wide enough to help serve the city's new multi-storey car park, which opened in 1969. The Whitefriars redevelopment scheme in the 2000s replaced the old multi-storey with one more, acceptably screened by new shop buildings.

STATION ROAD EAST

THE ONCE GRAND and prestigious town houses of Station Road East in June 1978. By this time, they had been blighted by the busy ring road immediately behind them and the intrusive

footbridge over it. Construction of the latter necessitated the demolition of one of the houses, thus bisecting the terrace. Station Road East had been created in 1860 to serve the new station of the London, Chatham and Dover Railway. The houses were built in the last quarter of the nineteenth century. *(Reproduced with kind permission of the* Kentish Gazette*)*

AN AMBITIOUS OFFICE development plan for this side of Station Road East blighted the late Victorian houses, and although the scheme was subsequently dropped, piecemeal demolition of the properties still continued in the late 1970s and into the early 1980s. Eventually, the whole area was cleared, and remained vacant until the early 1990s when the current scheme comprising both offices and flats emerged.

THE BAKER'S
TEMPERANCE HOTEL

THE BAKER'S TEMPERANCE Hotel, on the corner of St George's Street and Rose Lane, at the turn of the century (opposite). Not long before this picture was taken, the mainly seventeenth-century building had dummy Tudor-style timbers applied to its rendered façade. The genuine timbers of its structural framing were buried beneath the plaster work. Baker's Hotel transferred to a former private

house in Ivy Lane during the mid 1930s and its old premises were adapted to become the Parade Chambers. This was a collection of offices, small businesses and tea rooms, all housed under the same roof.

PARADE CHAMBERS WAS completely destroyed in the main Blitz of 1 June 1942. In the late 1940s, amateur archaeological trenches were sunk in the open cellars of the blitzed building and significant Roman finds were recorded. Ten years later, this stretch of Rose Lane (to the right of the photograph) was widened across the site of the lost building. Today, the old structure's rubble-filled cellars still exist beneath the modern roadway.

THE ROSE AND CROWN, ST DUNSTAN'S STREET

ST DUNSTAN'S STREET contains a wealth of lovely old timber-framed buildings, the best of which are the group on its south side. These three-storey double-jettied and multi-gabled structures date from the sixteenth and seventeenth centuries and include the famous House of Agnes inn. Another part contains a public house known in the 1940s as the Rose and Crown.

The old picture shows the effects of blast damage from a bomb that destroyed properties at the Station Road West junction opposite.
(Reproduced with kind permission of The Fisk Moore Collection)

DESPITE BOMBING IN both 1940 and 1942, which completely destroyed the buildings opposite it, the old Rose and Crown survived, even though it had to be repaired on more than one occasion. In more recent years, the pub fell victim to the trend for changing cherished pub names. Having been The Tap and Spile and then The Blind Dog, the old name has at last been restored.

THE ROYAL FOUNTAIN HOTEL, ST MARGARET'S STREET

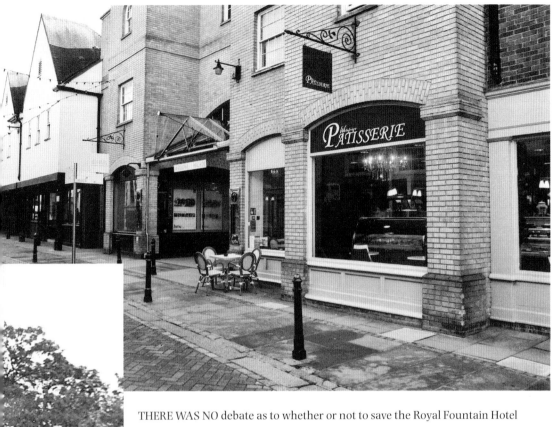

THERE WAS NO debate as to whether or not to save the Royal Fountain Hotel in St Margaret's Street following the Blitz, because it was utterly destroyed by firebombs in the early hours of 1 June 1942. The old photograph (left), taken a few days later, shows members of the armed forces clearing the debris of this once grand building. The hotel was neither rebuilt nor re-opened elsewhere. In the early post-war years, archaeologists dug in its complex of cellars before they were filled in and a car park was laid out.
(Reproduced with kind permission of Mr A. Moody)

IN THE EARLY post-war years, the site of the lost hotel was not redeveloped as it fell within the route reserved for the east to west cross-city relief road. The planned road was actually begun with the widening of Gravel Walk, but it went no further and the scheme was dropped in the late 1960s. Despite this, the Royal Fountain Hotel site remained a car park for another fifteen years. The present Marlowe Shopping Arcade was opened in the mid 1980s.

THE FLEUR DE LIS,
HIGH STREET

THE HIGH STREET lost some noted historic buildings in the 1950s. Among these was the famous Fleur de Lis hotel, pictured here in 1955 when its future was in serious doubt. On the surface is an eighteenth-century façade, largely of mathematical tiles, but beneath was an ancient structure with some sections dating back to the fourteenth century. The interior contained some superb wood panelling and an exquisite staircase, while the rear elevation displayed a jumble of timbered elevations and roof profiles.

THE EMPTY HOTEL was offered for sale in the mid 1950s and changed hands several times. It has been widely reported that at least one of the transient owners helped himself to the old building's many decorative

internal features. Eventually, demolition was proposed and, despite lobbying from a group of proto-city conservationists, the Fleur de Lis came down in March 1958. Interestingly, one old projecting window, complete with carved corbels, from the hotel's rear elevation, was saved and later reinstated in a building along nearby Whitehorse Lane.

THE MAN OF KENT,
WORTHGATE PLACE

THE MAN OF Kent public house, on the corner of Worthgate Place and Pin Hill (to the right of the photograph), in 1965. This interesting building, constructed in two distinct periods, dates from

the seventeenth century and has a nineteenth-century slate-roofed
pub extension. It was threatened with demolition for the second stage
of the ring road, in the course of which Pin Hill would become a dual
carriageway. In the event, only the nineteenth-century addition was
pulled down, and the original part later reverted to a house.
(Reproduced with kind permission of Edward Wilmot)

WITH THE GENERAL decline in the number of city pubs, already well
underway by the 1960s, those lost to both road building and slum
clearance schemes were not replaced. However, the name Man of
Kent was retained and transferred to the nearby Station Hotel. Sadly,
however, this was later renamed The Roundhouse and has now closed
altogether, as the disappearance of public houses continues apace.

KNOTTS LANE

KNOTTS LANE. A minor thoroughfare of very humble dwellings in the early 1930s when the whole area was being considered for slum clearance. This was as a direct result of the setting up of the City Council Housing Committee in 1925 and the establishment of new council housing estates on the city outskirts over the following ten years. The ancient houses, dominated by the three-storey double-jettied and gabled seventeenth-century house at No. 22 (to the left of the photograph opposite), were mostly taken down in 1937 and 1938.
(Reproduced with kind permission of Dr William Urry)

THE CLEARED WEST side of Knotts Lane became a scrapyard almost straight away and remained in use as such until the late 1960s. It was thought that a section of the scrapyard's perimeter wall had survived from the medieval Black Prince's Chantry in nearby King Street. The area finally underwent a return to residential use from the early 1970s onwards. The ultimate fate of the old wall is not known.

OLD RUTTINGTON LANE

THE MOSTLY SEVENTEENTH-CENTURY cottages of Old Ruttington Lane, seen from the junction with Broad Street in the early 1930s (right). Many of these small dwellings were well constructed and did not feature in the slum clearance programmes of the 1920s and '30s. No. 55, the home of Alice Blackman, was entirely brick built and carried a date stone of 1688. Sadly, the Blitz ravaged the lane and Granny Blackman lost her little house.

IN THE EARLY post-war years, prefabricated school buildings were erected on the south side of Old Ruttington Lane and across the site of the lost cottages. The prefabs are still there today and are just visible in the modern photograph on the left. The building in the foreground (to the right of the photograph), at the junction with Broad Street, is a replacement for the one lost in the Blitz.

ST PETER'S LANE

THREE EARLY EIGHTEENTH-CENTURY cottages at Nos 62, 64 and 66 St Peter's Lane, in about 1935, having just been identified as part of 'Slum Clearance Area No. 11'. As with most of the

ancient dwellings in this lane, they were of very cheap construction, being made of brick only in the lower storey of the front elevation. The remainder would have been poor timber framing hidden by weather boarding, tiles, or in this case, pebble dashing. Houses on the east side of the lane, including these, backed onto a common yard containing the privies, washing lines and a huge iron mangle.
(*Reproduced with kind permission of Canterbury Museums*)

THE OLD ST PETER'S Lane cottages were demolished in 1937 and 1938, along with scores of other similar examples. In the early post-war years, prefabricated school buildings were erected along a section of the lane's eastern frontage. The prefabs are still there, as per the current view, although they have not recently been in use. Redevelopment of the site is likely in the near future.

MILL LANE AND KING STREET

MILL LANE (RIGHT), seen from across King Street, in 1964. The cottages, at Nos 19–21, date from the second quarter of the nineteenth century. Other houses on the corner site had been demolished some time before. During the year this picture was taken, the Blackfriars area of Canterbury, encompassing Blackfriars Street, King Street and Mill Lane, was identified for slum clearance and redevelopment. However, by this time, local conservationists had found a voice and protests were lodged.

(Reproduced with kind permission of of Mr R.E. Cranfield)

DESPITE THE WELL-ORGANISED protest, and a sympathetic official ear, this was not enough to prevent many of the old houses in both Mill Lane and King Street from subsequently being demolished. A neo-Georgian housing development had appeared across much of the site by the late 1960s. This scheme was dubbed a 'miniature Chelsea' by its critics, although the houses have since found much favour.

BARRETTS' MOTORS,
ST PETER'S STREET

IN 1930S CANTERBURY, shops constructed in the modern International Style were few and far between. One of the best was the new Barretts shop in St Peter's Street. It is pictured here shortly

after opening on 18 March 1938. Only four months before, their previous shop on the site had been burnt out. Designed by architect H. Campbell Ashenden, the façade was finished in bronze and Roman marble and the central arcade allowed a generous window display area.
(Reproduced with kind permission of Barretts' Motors)

SADLY, BARRETTS' PRESTIGIOUS new building was itself badly damaged by fire in a late wartime raid on Canterbury during January 1944. In fact, the entire premises were all but wiped out by that single incendiary bomb dropped during the raid. What was left of their 1930s building was patched up and survived through to the late 1970s, when Barretts redeveloped much of their St Peter's Street frontage.

THE POST-WAR LONGMARKET

THE OLD VIEW from 1955 shows the prefabricated shops on the Longmarket site, shortly
after Mr R.E. Cranfield had set up the Camera Shop (left). He had come to Canterbury in 1953

and for two years ran a professional studio at No. 8 High Street. In 1959, the Longmarket site was cleared prior to redevelopment. The Camera Shop was the last prefab left standing as Mr Cranfield could not find new premises. Fortunately, he was eventually able to move into a former sweet shop at No. 43 Burgate. As his business expanded, Cranfield took over two local firms, namely Fisk-Moore and Photocentre, then also opened a hi-fi shop in Burgate and an optical shop in Butchery Lane.
(Reproduced with kind permission of Mr R.E. Cranfield)

A MODERNIST LONGMARKET scheme replaced the prefabs in 1961, and is featured elsewhere in the book, as it too has since been consigned to history. As for the subsequent activities of Cranfield's, the mid- to late-1990s recession, coupled with extortionate rents, forced the family firm to scale down to the one camera shop, which was owned outright by them. When Mr R.E. Cranfield finally retired, his daughter Sarah took over the shop for a brief period, before selling up for good.

ABBOTTS MILL,
ST RADIGUND'S STREET

DOMINATING THE CITY skyline, second only to the cathedral, was Abbotts Mill, seen from St Radigund's Street in the early 1920s (left). This six-storey timber-framed structure was designed by John Smeaton (also responsible for the Eddystone Lighthouse) and built in 1792. In the 1880s, the mill was owned by famous Canterbury artist Thomas Sidney Cooper, together with the nearby Westgate Mill. The mill was utterly destroyed in a spectacular and memorable blaze on 17 October 1933.

THE SITE OF Abbotts Mill has remained undeveloped ever since the building's dramatic destruction by fire: a process that lasted some three days. Today, the mill races can still be seen, together with a few structural iron pieces that are still *in situ*. On warm summer evenings, drinkers from the nearby Miller's Arms pub continue to enjoy the area.

THE PRIORY, LADY WOOTTON'S GREEN

THE PRIORY WAS a seventeenth-century L-shaped house that stood on the
northern corner of Broad Street at its junction with Lady Wootton's Green.
The old picture dates from 1910. The timber-framed jettied upper storey is
clad in mathematical tiles to imitate brick, while the lower storey is built in
brick and Caen stone blocks. The stone, together with other architectural
features, had been plundered from the ruins of nearby St Augustine's Abbey.
The house was tidied up between the wars, losing much of its character in
the process.

LADY WOOTTON'S GREEN suffered considerably in the main Blitz of 1 June 1942. Only one building escaped any significant damage. The Priory itself had some roof damage caused by an incendiary bomb, and this was enough to justify complete demolition of this attractive and historic building. Diocesan House, built in the Dean and Chapter's then much-favoured neo-Georgian style, appeared on the site in 1955. An extension to the building (seen beyond) was added in the late 1980s.

ST MARY BREDIN CHURCH, ROSE LANE

THE CENTRAL AISLE of St Mary Bredin church, looking towards the altar, in the early years of the twentieth century. Built in 1868, it replaced a smaller medieval church on the same site.

The Victorian church was noted for its octagonal tower and spire, a prominent feature of pre-war cityscapes. The church was gutted in the main Blitz of June 1942 and demolished in the months that followed. The last traces of it finally disappeared in 1952, when Rose Lane alongside was considerably widened. A replacement church was built on a different site in 1957.
(Reproduced with kind permission of Frank Bailey)

BACK ON THE old Rose Lane site, the west ends of both medieval and Victorian churches were uncovered in an archaeological dig during 1980, prior to the construction of the Marlowe Shopping Arcade. The church's east end, where the altar once stood, has long since been buried beneath the modern carriageway (now Rose Square). Today, the new Whitefriars scheme has replaced the previous collection of late 1960s and early 1970s modernist buildings in this area.

ST GEORGE'S CHURCH, ST GEORGE'S STREET

THE SHELL OF St George's church in the main street (opposite). The old picture shows damage caused by incendiary bombs in the main Blitz of 1 June 1942, as well as by the local authority's attempt to pull down the entire remains. The demolition was halted by Canon Crum, who recognised the historical significance of the building (the lower part of the tower dates from the twelfth century). The shell lingered on until the early 1950s, with plans for its future swinging between its complete retention as a war memorial to its complete demolition for road widening and shopping space. *(Reproduced with kind permission of RCHM England)*

IN 1952, A compromise was eventually reached. This allowed the tower of St George's to remain, while the rest of the church, largely a Victorian rebuild, was finally

swept away. The topmost part of the tower, demolished in 1942, was reinstated and the rest of the structure carefully restored. Today, the 'clock' tower is a familiar and much-loved landmark, although it is now somewhat overshadowed by the over-scale Fenwick's store opposite.

THE PRE-WAR LONGMARKET

THE WONDERFUL REGENCY Corn Exchange and Longmarket building was undoubtedly one of those Blitz-damaged landmarks in Canterbury that could have been restored, had there

been the will to do so. Despite some fire damage, the basic structure remained sound with little evidence of even a scorch mark on the beautiful St George's Street elevation. Nevertheless, most of the building was demolished during the second week of June 1942, a process that had just begun in the old picture. Prefabricated shops appeared on the site in 1947.

(Reproduced with kind permission of Mr A. Moody)

EVEN AFTER THE prefab shops had appeared here in the late 1940s, significant surviving elements of the old Regency Corn Exchange and Longmarket building could be found on the site, right up until the late 1950s. These finally disappeared when the prefabs themselves were dismantled. The modernist Longmarket development, which is featured elsewhere in this book, was opened in 1961. Largely unloved, this somewhat box-like scheme lasted for only thirty years. Today's Longmarket buildings date from the early 1990s.

WATLING STREET

THE IVY-CLAD SHELLS of two brick Jacobean houses of 1625 on the
north side of Watling Street. The old picture was taken in 1953, just
prior to their demolition. Gutted by incendiary bombs in June 1942,
recognition of their true historic worth prevented demolition at the time,
which was a remarkable achievement given the lack of concern for such
factors elsewhere in the city. Far from being empty ruins, an office existed
on the ground floor of No. 19 (to the right of the photograph) beneath a
temporary roof constructed within the shell.

THE REASON FOR the decision to demolish this romantic-looking ruin
in 1953 is not clear, for the site was not redeveloped again for nearly
twenty years. In fact, during the interim period, it became a small parking
area. The present office scheme has successfully mimicked the scale and
proportions of the surviving Jacobean building to its right, which is visible
in both views.

ST ANDREW'S CHURCH, WINCHEAP GREEN

DESTRUCTION OF SIGNIFICANT and much-loved Canterbury landmarks continued right up to the early 1970s. One of the last to perish was St Andrew's Presbyterian church at Wincheap Green, pictured here just before demolition in 1973. Designed by city architect John Green Hall and built

in red brick with stone dressing, this lovely church opened for worship in
1881. It became redundant in the mid 1960s and faced an uncertain future.
It was demolished for a building scheme that never materialised.
(Reproduced with kind permission of the Kentish Gazette*)*

THE DERELICT AND overgrown site of St Andrew's church, enclosed by
high hoardings, was still vacant some twenty years later. In fact, during this
time, closer inspection revealed that substantial sections of the church's
basement, or crypt walls, still existed (a picture of these can be seen in
Canterbury's Lost Heritage). Today's mixed development appeared across the
site in the early 1990s.

THE MODERNIST LONGMARKET

THE MODERN LONGMARKET development of 1960, as seen from Rose Lane in March 1967. This had replaced prefabricated shops on the site that had in turn been erected on the site of blitzed buildings, including the Corn Exchange. The 1960 scheme had been specially designed to allow unobstructed views of the cathedral, as the old picture clearly illustrates. Unfortunately, the box-like appearance of this development, without much detail, meant that it earned few friends.

(Reproduced with kind permission of the Kentish Gazette)

THE UNLOVED MODERNIST Longmarket scheme was demolished in 1990, heralding an extensive archaeological investigation of the whole area. Sadly, a misguided campaign halted the City Council's plans to rebuild the pre-war Corn Exchange and Longmarket building – featured elsewhere in this book – on the grounds that they wanted an open space retained in the new scheme. Today's overscale pastiche development does indeed have an open space, but decent views of the cathedral are no longer possible.

CANTERBURY EAST STATION

CANTERBURY EAST STATION approach, coal yard and goods sidings, as they were in September 1955. The picture was taken to record a derailment caused during shunting manoeuvres.

Railway men can be seen inspecting the errant carriage. Numerous changes to the scene have occurred over the years. The dilapidated train shed, spanning the main line in the distance, was demolished and replaced by modern platform shelters in 1958.
(Reproduced with kind permission of the Kentish Gazette)

CANTERBURY EAST SAW its last steam-hauled service train in May 1959. Then in the 1960s, local railway freight traffic gradually transferred to the roads and the new motorway network, as Dr Beeching's pro-road agenda took shape. The sidings at Canterbury East went out of use and were eventually lifted. Those on the 'down' or Dover side of the station, as seen here, have since been replaced by the station car park.

BUS STATION,
ST GEORGE'S LANE

THE EARLY POST-WAR years saw an increase in bus travel, caused by various factors. These included the establishment of new out-of-town housing estates and schools, as well as the closure of some secondary railways. Bus design also underwent changes, not least of which was an increase in width and length. By the early 1950s, Canterbury's small bus station in St Peter's Place had become inadequate and many services operated from overflow positions in Station Road West. Consequently, a large new station was opened in St George's Lane during May 1956 and is pictured here during its first year.

THE HEYDAY OF bus travel in the 1950s was short-lived, as the nation moved inexorably towards universal car ownership. Local city services, which could once easily justify a double-decker, had given over entirely to minibuses by the 1980s. The bus station itself was extensively remodelled in the early 2000s, as part of the adjacent Whitefriars development scheme. The current view (left), taken on a Sunday, shows far fewer buses than one would normally encounter here on a typical weekday.

CAR PARK, NORTH LANE

A LOVELY PICTURE of North Lane car park in December 1958, not long after it had been expanded onto the site of demolished buildings. In the foreground can be seen a Ford Consul, a Standard Vanguard 10, Hillman Minx and an elderly Ford Anglia. The registration numbers would suggest that these vehicles were owned by local people. At this time, the limited number of tourists to the city usually arrived by train or coach.

(Reproduced with kind permission of the Kentish Gazette*)*

NORTH LANE CAR park is still in use today, although its conversion into an extension of the Westgate Gardens was briefly considered

in the 1980s. Inevitably, cars parked here these days will often carry European plates, and British-made vehicles are very much in the minority. The old cottages, in the background of both views, were once threatened by the ring road third stage, but were renovated after that scheme was cancelled in 1975.

COACH PARK, LONGPORT

A WONDERFUL PANORAMIC view of Longport Coach Park, as
it was in June 1961. The site is crowded with coaches exclusively
from the Home Counties, including a number from the local B.E.T.
(British Electric Traction) companies of East Kent and Maidstone and
District. At this time, the park could also be used by cars, not that
there is any room for them on this day! By the mid 1970s, the first
coaches from Europe had arrived.
(Reproduced with kind permission of the Kentish Gazette)

IN 1974 AND 1975, Longport Coach Park was expanded by the
demolition of the adjacent premises of Amey's Blinds (in an

old Malthouse) and a terrace of late Georgian cottages known as Union Row, both of which can
be seen in the old view. Today, the coach park has moved to Northgate, and the Longport site is
entirely given over to cars, including residents' spaces.

GRAVEL WALK

CANTERBURY'S POST-WAR ROAD plans encouraged the movement of cars into and through the city. Ultimately, four inner-city multi-storey car parks were planned, but as an interim measure, vast amounts of surface car parking had to be provided. The old view shows acres of such temporary parking in Gravel Walk during the mid 1960s. Simon Langton School once stood on the site to the right. In the event, only one multi-storey was built, that on the south (left) side of Gravel Walk in 1969.

(Reproduced with kind permission of Ben May)

GRAVEL WALK WENT from being a narrow wall-lined lane in 1959 to a dual carriageway by the early 1960s. The cross-city relief road, of which it would have formed part, was never completed. This left a somewhat incongruous expanse of tarmac, until the Whitefriars area was comprehensively redeveloped in the early 2000s. Today, Gravel Walk has another identity, as a pedestrian-only shopping street, as can be seen in the current view.

Other titles published by The History Press

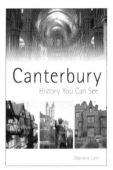

Canterbury: History You Can See
MARJORIE LYLE

A day trip to Canterbury can feel like being 'punch drunk'. Sometimes there is too much history to see. Great buildings like cathedrals can dwarf their neighbours and smother the memory of their various builders. This book introduces the builders, traders, craftsmen and saints and sinners who created Canterbury during its long history and tells many surprising stories about the people behind the buildings.

978 0 7524 4538 0

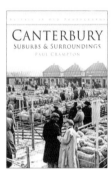

Canterbury: Suburbs & Surroundings
PAUL CRAMPTON

Canterbury is so much more than the small area enclosed by what remains of its ancient city walls. During Roman times, for example, when the city wall first appeared, the areas occupied by today's suburbs were used as burial grounds. This book shows us the changing shape of these suburbs during the twentieth century as they developed into what we know today.

978 0 7524 5572 3

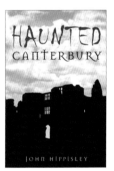

Haunted Canterbury
JOHN HIPPISLEY

Journey through the dark side of Canterbury, a medieval city steeped in history and ghostly goings-on. A designated Ancient World Heritage site with numerous old landmarks, Canterbury is riddled with countless tales of ghosts and hauntings. This chilling selection of mysterious happenings will captivate anyone interested in discovering the ghosts of Canterbury. It will also serve as an ideal guide or lasting souvenir of the author's renowned ghost tour.

978 0 7524 4998 2

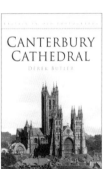

Canterbury Cathedral
DEREK BUTLER

Canterbury Cathedral in Old Photographs records the living history of this incredible architectural treasure. The author has selected images from private archives to highlight the many stunning architectural features. This book shows the importance of the building for local residents and its significance to our national heritage.

978 0 7524 4961 6

Visit our website and discover thousands of other History Press books.

www.thehistorypress.co.uk